Ethnographic Terminalia: Washington, D.C. 2014
The Bureau of Memories: Archives & Ephemera
Hierarchy Gallery

Published by the Society for Visual Anthropology, a section of the American Anthropological Association. 2300 Clarendon Blvd., Suite 1301. Arlington, VA 22201

The review essay in this volume was originally published as "The Bureau of Memories: Archives and Ephemera." Fieldsights - Visual and New Media Review, Cultural Anthropology Online, March 20, 2015, http://www.culanth.org/fieldsights/647-the-bureau-of-memories-archives-and-ephemera. Our grateful acknowledgement to the editors.

Edited by Ethnographic Terminalia:
Craig Campbell, Kate Hennessy, Fiona P. McDonald,
Trudi Lynn Smith, Stephanie Takaragawa, Tom Miller

Lead editors and print design: Kate Hennessy and Rachel Topham

Exhibition Photography: Trudi Lynn Smith

Cover Design: Ethnographic Terminalia, Rachel Topham and
Ian Kirkpatrick

ISBN 978-1-931303-48-4

Washington, D.C. 2014:

Contributors

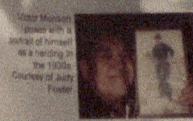

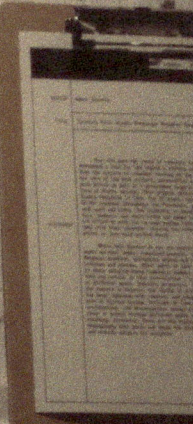

This installation invites you to feel history. **Please Touch.**

♦ Sort archival documents
♦ Flip through photos
♦ Handle reindeer products
♦ Listen to speakers share their memories.

Stories of people, places, animals, and events overlap visually, tactilely, and audibly, inviting you to reflect on how words, objects, and voices invoke emotions at the same time as they convey information. **How do you feel this history?**

Amber Lincoln
University of Alaska Fairbanks
aalincoln@uaf.edu

Installation view of Amber Lincoln's *History Felt*

Ethnographic Terminalia

Washington D.C. 2014:
The Bureau of Memories: Archives and Ephemera

Hierarchy Gallery

Curated by
Ethnographic Terminalia
Craig Campbell
Kate Hennessy
Fiona P. McDonald
Trudi Lynn Smith
Stephanie Takaragawa

with guest curator
Thomas Ross Miller

Exhibition Photography
Trudi Lynn Smith

Acknowledgements

Generous support for the Bureau of Memories: Archives & Ephemera
exhibition comes from the American Anthropological Association, the Society
for Visual Anthropology, and the Edward S. and Joyce I. Miller Charitable Trust.
We are also grateful to the Department of Anthropology at the University of
Texas at Austin, Department of Anthropology at University College London,
Chapman University, Berkeley College School of Liberal Arts, and the School of
Interactive Arts and Technology at Simon Fraser University.

Ethnographic Terminalia recognizes Arjun Shankar for his role as a
collaborating curator of four works from CAMRA.

The Curatorial Collective extends special thanks to: Jessica Eley, Meghan
Dunwoodie, Brent Sipes, Sara Gore, No Kings Collective, James Kerns,
Corehaus DC, Brandon Hill, Peter Chang, Sarah Petersen, Dana Powell, Ivy
Mansion, David Goren, Lina Dib, Aynur Kadir, Rachel Topham, Erin Boyd,
Sara Perry, Jonathan Marion, Jason Watkins, Ed Liebow, Rachel Watkins, Mary
Gray, Joslyn Osten and Rachel Ward.

Finally, we'd like to express our gratitude to all of the participating
anthropologists, researchers, and artists for the 2014 exhibition.

Ethnographic Terminalia 2014
Washington DC

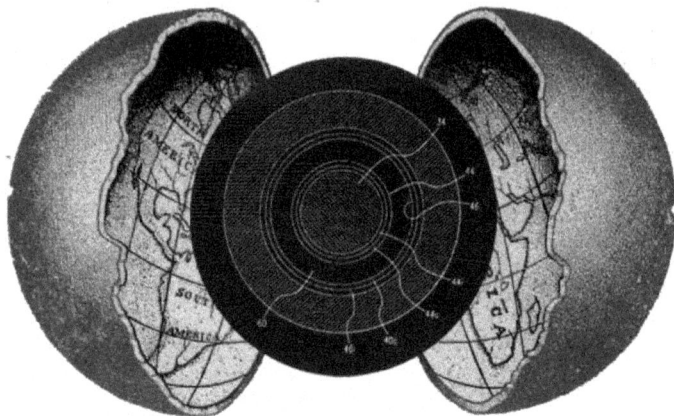

The Bureau of Memories
Archives & Ephemera

Washington D.C. 2014:
The Bureau of Memories: Archives and Ephemera

The Bureau of Memories: Archives & Ephemera was an immersive installation held in tandem with the 113th annual meeting of the American Anthropological Association. Featuring dozens of works engaged with archival memories, the exhibition invited visitors to encounter voices and images from the past in a 21st-century technological space. Artists and anthropologists re-imagined and remixed 20th-century media including 16mm film, short-wave radio, land-line telephones, photogravure and paper documents.

For the exhibition in 2014 Ethnographic Terminalia created a mythopoetic archival institution called "The Bureau of Memories." We designed this exhibition as a curated gallery of items from the vast archives of this bureau. Each item in the Bureau's "Archives and Ephemera" show was catalogued and exhibited at Hierarchy, a gallery and event space on Columbia Road in Washington, DC.

The Bureau of Memories: Archives and Ephemera reflects on the archive and its discontents. Where there is history, there is haunting. This exhibition was an effort to re-imagine and reposition archives as sites which have the capacity to generate significant gaps and blind spots as well as produce contested historical memories. The installation was designed to draw out anthropology's uncanny, unnerving, and ephemeral specters, reinterpreting archives not only as repositories of information but as generators of absence and obscurity. *The Bureau of Memories* explored residual media technologies and aesthetics alongside public memory and official histories. We sought to disaggregate nostalgia for strange and dusty forms from living historical frameworks, foregrounding sensorial attunements and evoking the passage of time in history and politics.

Amidst the proliferation of information, screens, and virtual realities, history continues to haunt the present as specters of the past appear in the guise of digitized traces. Yet many analog collections built to preserve information and knowledge are becoming lost in the digital age. With this loss other forms

General installation view, Washington, DC, 2014

emerge in a perpetual reconfiguration of archival order as a bricolage of residual media, analog devices, documents and digitized copies. Documents of everyday life consigned to banality, but also strangely incongruous items that fit poorly with established or emerging narratives, point to fissures in the structuring of historical memory. In *The Bureau of Memories* archives were conceptualized as sites of both official records and broken fragments.

The international array of works on display included prints, projections, sculpture, performance, textiles, video, and sonic artifacts from wax-cylinder field recordings and classic African radio broadcasts to a 3D-rendered audio spectrogram of the famous 18½-minute gap in the Watergate tapes. Some artists and collaborators directly engaged with archives and archival research, while others commented on the structure of information management, the resonance of public memory and forgetting, and the politics of voice and visibility.

Two special projects within the *Bureau of Memories* include the invited exhibition of works by artists and collaborators associated with CAMRA and a series of collaborative works organized by Tom Miller and Craig Campbell under the title *The Schizophonic Archive.*

Ethnographic Terminalia often collaborates with local groups and organizations in an effort to expand our curatorial vision and voice. For the 2014 exhibition we approached the anthropologist John L. Jackson with an invitation to participate in *The Bureau of Memories*. It was this connection that led us to partner up with University of Pennsylvania's CAMRA initiative, under the lead of Arjun Shankar. CAMRA installed four different works in *The Bureau of Memories: Bad Friday, REACH in Ambler, Sweet Tea*, and *The Ward.*

The Schizophonic Archive's project within the *Bureau of Memories* made use of publicly available archival audio recordings. Poaching the term 'schizophonia' from the sound theorist R. Murray Shafer, we drew attention to the split experience that describes a person listening to a trace of the past in the present, out of time and place. By repositioning these recordings we sought to match new audiences with old voices and to encourage a sensuous appreciation of these temporally and spatially dislocated sonic rarities.

~ Ethnographic Terminalia with Guest Curator Thomas R. Miller.

General installation view, Washington, DC, 2014

General installation view, Washington, DC, 2014

You can't study Rasta from outside. If you are not Rasta you

General installation view, Washington, DC, 2014

HIERARCHY

THE BUREAU OF MEMORIES: ARCHIVES AND EPHEMERA

Paul Stoller

For the Songhay people of the Republics of Niger and Mali in West Africa history is more than a series of dead words on a page that recount the stories of the past. For them, history is also a set of ever-living forces that sensuously bring the past into the dynamic flow of contemporary life.

The great reigns of fifteenth- and sixteenth-century Songhay kings (the dynasty of the Askias) are indeed recounted in two historical texts written in the seventeenth century, Mohammed es-Saadi's Tarikh al-Soudan and Mahmoud Kati's Tarikh al-Fattach. These texts describe imperial governance, royal rivalries, political tensions, and great military exercises. These invaluable works, however, do not dwell on the texture of social life. How did sixteenth- and seventeenth-century Songhay people cope with the vicissitudes of an unpredictable climate that powerfully dictated the health and well-being of urban and rural populations? Would the spirits bring rains in a given year or would they ensure yet another season of drought, yet another period of hunger and suffering? How did the people of that time adjust to incessant warfare, let alone the expansion of Islam? How did these powerful forces shape the quality of social life?

These existential questions introduce us to histories "from below" that are not often articulated on the pages of a book that resides in an classic library; rather, they are evoked in rituals like spirit possession during which words, music,

Reprinted with permission. Stoller, Paul. "The Bureau of Memories: Archives and Ephemera." Fieldsights - Visual and New Media Review, Cultural Anthropology Online, March 20, 2015, http://www.culanth.org/fieldsights/647-the-bureau-of-memories-archives-and-ephemera

Facing page, exhibition entrance. *The Bureau of Memories: Archives and Ephemera*, Washington, DC, 2014

Installation view of Christian S. Hammons's *In Animate: A Multispecies Ethnography*

movement, and smell sweep the sensuous past into the vibrant present. The old words of incantations and praise-poetry speak to the existential relations of past and present. The sound of the monochord violin "cries" for ancestral recognition such that the links between past and present might be restored. The danced movements of spirit mediums evoke the mythic stories of the "distant past." The smells of Bint-al Sudan provoke the onset of possession, a truly dramatic transformation that sensuously compresses past and present. In the moment of possession historical, social and cultural memory converge in the body of the medium. It is a moment when the forces of the cosmos speak truth to power and bear witness to the challenges of living in the world.

For many peoples there is a tactile dimension to history in which memories are brought to life in multifaceted archival arenas. These are arenas in which people are able to hear, smell, and touch the past—activities that bring distant time instinctually into the present.

One of the great challenges for contemporary ethnographers and artists, then, is to re-awaken our tactile sense of the past, to create multi-sensorial spaces in which the stories of the past are told and retold, understood and comprehended

General installation view, Washington, DC, 2014

Installation view of camra's *Sweet Tea*

anew through prisms of sound, scent, movement, and touch. The multi-modal installations that comprised the seventh Ethnographic Terminalia, The Bureau of Memories: Archives and Ephemera met this contemporary representational challenge—and did so admirably through twenty-six thought-provoking and boundary-challenging "historical" works.

As a curated collection the installation wonders "what lies beyond and what lies within disciplinary territories. The terminus is the end the boundary and the border; it is also a beginning, its own place, a site of experience and encounter" (Ethnographic Terminalia Collective 2014, i). In The Bureau of Memories, artists and anthropologists re-imagine and remix twentieth-century media including 16mm film, short-wave radio, land-line telephones, photogravure, and paper documents, all of which invite

> visitors to encounter voices and images from the past in a
> technological space that is both historical and contemporary.
> ... The Bureau of Memories considers archives as sites
> of official records and broken fragments. Bureaucratically
> mundane and incongruously playful items slip through the
> cracks of established narratives, pointing toward fissures in
> the structures of historical memory. The installation draws out
> anthropology's uncanny specters, reinterpreting archives not
> only as repositories of information but as generators of absence
> and obscurity.

Here are some examples from a few of the works that comprised The Bureau of Memories: "REACH in Ambler" is an installation about the asbestos producing factory community of Ambler which is located near Philadelphia. The installation evokes questions of governmentality, community organizing, and how decisions are made—to close the asbestos factory. The five-minute filmlet, based on interviews, oral histories, tours, and field research "explores the boundaries between methodology, empiricism, and research reflexivity as they converge in visual media" (Tarditi, Zuberi and Ziv. Ibid. 5). Put another way, through image and sound this installation explores the spaces between things.

The same can be said of "The Ward: Dubois and Oral Histories," an installation that features an interactive space "for users to 'play' board games as they watch and hear about the life of civil rights activists from the Seventh War (Philadelphia) community. By thinking outside the book and even outside of the film we seek to think about the many ways that learning (i.e. kinesthetic, audiovisual, etc.) can occur and the differential possibilities which tactile interaction might provide for active engagement with 'lived' histories" (Brodie, Hillier and Laughlin 2014, Ibid. 7). Here again the installation takes us "between" learning modalities.

The tactility of history is also showcased in Amber Lincoln's "History Felt: Alaska Peninsula Reindeer Herding," a history patched together from "memos, rangeland permits, and maps housed in the U.S. National Archives, historical photos and tools in individual collections and museums." Here the history of reindeer herding is constructed from the "design of documents, the texture of objects, and the rhythm of voices" that one can hear see and feel while seated on a reindeer pelted installation chair—a point of reception for the multi-modal telling and re-telling stories (Lincoln 2014 Ibid, 15). Here again the installation takes us to a bridge that spans the spaces between past and present, between being-there and being-here.

Space precludes a description of the twenty-three other evocative multi-sensory installations in The Bureau Memories, each of which singularly explores the existential boundaries of past and present. In those installations, ethnographers and artists employed a variety of media, artistic techniques, and machines (film, video, photography, photoetchings, and digital imagery, recordings, audio-photo series, re-mixing and reinventing sound, sound machines, ecstatic truths and translation, and photoboxes) to probe the outer reaches of our historical and symbolic imagination.

Put in a slightly different language, The Bureau of Memory is an embodied exploration of what medieval Sufi mystics like Ibn al' Arabi called "the between"—indeterminate spaces that are neither here nor there. For him, the between is

> something that separates . . . two other things, while never
> going to one side . . . as, for example, the line that separates
> shadow from sun light. God says, "he let forth this two seas
> that meet together, between them a barzakh they do not
> overpass" (Koroan 55:19); in other words one sea does not

mix with the other . . . any two adjacent things are in need
of barzakh, which is neither one nor the other but which
possesses the power . . . of both. The barzakh is something
that separates a known from an unknown, an existent from a
non-existent, a negated from an affirmed, an intelligible from
a non-intelligible. (Crapanzano 2003, 57–58; see also Chittick
1989; Stoller 2008)

In the mystical world of the Sufis, the spaces between things are indeterminate.
For them, it is the indeterminacy of these spaces that fires our imagination. The
between, then, is a challengingly liminal place where we innovate and invent. As
demonstrated in installations that constitute The Bureau of Memories, it is in
liminal spaces that we blend elements—poised on the barzakh—to refashion the
world and unleash some of its wonders. As Crapanzano (2003, 58) notes:

The liminal has often been likened to the dream. . . . It suggests
imaginative possibilities that are not necessarily available to
us in everyday life. Through paradox, ambiguity, contradiction,
bizarre, exaggerated, and at times grotesque symbols—masks,
costumes and figurines—and the evocation of transcendent
realities mystery and supernatural powers, the liminal offers us
a view of the world to which we are normally blinded by the
usual structures of social and cultural life.

In our disciplinary corner of the world, we have written a great deal about
ethnographic representation—writing about writing. There has also been much
recent debate about the social challenges of the Anthropocene as well as the
twists and turns of ontology in social description. No matter the turn of these
debates, they have usually consisted of linear arguments presented in a textual
format—all in search for what John Dewey (1929) long ago called "the quest
for certainty." The format of these arguments has often taken us away from the
murky, creative spaces between things.

Enter The Bureau of Memories. With its inclusively tactile and multi-sensorial
dimensions, the exhibition demonstrates the central importance of a new wave of
anthropological expression, an articulation that fuses past and present and here
and there. In short, The Bureau of Memories invites us to glimpse into the future
and provides a much-appreciated tonic for our discipline.

General installation view, Washington, DC, 2014

References

Brodie, Stephanie, Amy Hiller and Corrina Laughlin. 2014. "The Ward: Dubois and Oral Histories." The Bureau of Memories: Archives and Ephemera. Installation catelogue. Washington D.C.

Chittick, William C. 1989. The Sufi Path of Knowledge: Ibn al-Arabi's Metaphysics of Imagination. Albany, N.Y.: SUNY Press.

Crapanzano, Vincent. 2003. Imaginative Horizons: An Essay in Literary-Philosophical Anthropology. Chicago: University of Chicago Press.

Dewey, John. 1929. The Quest for Certainty: A Study of the Relation of Knowledge and Action. New York: Minton, Balch.

Es-Saadi, Mohammed. 1900. Tarikh es Soudan. Translated by O. Houdas. Paris: Leroux.

Ethnographic Terminalia Curatorial Collective. 2014. The Bureau of Memories: Archives and Ephemera. Installation catelogue. Washington D.C.

Kati, Mahmoud. 1913. Tarikh al-Fattach. Translated by M. Delafosse. Paris: Maissoneuve.

Lincoln, Amber. 2014. "History Felt: Alaska Peninsula Reindeer Herding." The Bureau of Memories: Archives and Ephemera. Installation catelogue. Washington D.C.

Stoller, Paul. 2008. The Power of the Between: An Anthropological Odyssey. Chicago: University of Chicago Press.

Tarditi, Matthew, Jabari Zuberi and Tali Ziv. 2014. "REACH: In Ambler (REACH= Resources for Education and Action for Community Health). The Bureau of Memories: Archives and Ephemera. Installation catelogue. Washington D.C.

General installation view, Washington, DC, 2014

Installation view of Lina Dib's contribution to *The Schizophonic Archive*

Installation view of Kwame Phillips and Debra Spitulnik Vidali's
*Kabusha Radio Remix: Your Questions Answered by Pioneering
Zambian Talk Show Host, David Yumba (1923-1990)*, 2014

Installation view of Alejandro Luperca Morales's
Post Meridiem/ Post Mortem

camra
Bad Friday Goes to Africa

In August of 2012, Arjun Shankar and Mariam Durrani accompanied Dr. John Jackson and Dr. Deborah Thomas from the University of Pennsylvania, Cape Town filmmaker Kurt Orderson of Azania Rising Productions, the Rasta band Ancient Vibrations and Rasta elders to screen the film *Bad Friday* to the Rasta diaspora in three cities: London, Cape Town, and Johannesburg." Mariam and Arjun collaborated on documenting the journey including the films "Beating as One: The Music of Ancient Vibrations" and "Rasta Rights and Reparations: Bad Friday Tour."

This installation seeks to create a novel sensory re-creation of the journey, juxtaposing photographs from the events with scrolling transcriptions of community member commentary and audio footage from the Ancient Vibrations musical performances. Together these pieces provide partial perspectives on how we make sense of transnational movements of people and ideas, with a specific focus on how diverse sensory processes challenge perceptions and normative representations of Rastafarian life, values, and culture.

camra
REACH in Ambler
(REACH = Resources for Education and Action for Community Health)

The borough of Ambler is a small community located outside of Philadelphia, Pennsylvania. In 1881, the Keasbey and Mattison Company, relocating from nearby Philadelphia, opened factories in Ambler to begin manufacturing asbestos in the form of roof tiles, insulation and brake linings. The production of the fibrous mineral quickly became the central economic activity and identifying characteristic of this "factory town." For almost one hundred years Ambler was an international locus for the production of asbestos (1880 to 1970), passing from one company to another until the harmful health effects of asbestos became widely known and factories subsequently closed their doors. Leaving in its wake was not only a massive environmental hazard and but also a deeply wounded community. The industrial legacy of asbestos production still greatly impacts residents today.

Based on in-depth interviews, oral histories, guided tours, and field research our first filmic product seeks to capture some of the initial questions at the heart of the project around governmentality, community engagement, and decision-making. Additionally, we strive to represent the multiperspectival realities, experiences and histories of Ambler and its residents around perceptions of perceived risk vs. actual risk, environmental justice, fear, social responsibility and community/civic engagement and communication. The project pivots on critical reflection that explores the boundaries between methodology, empiricism and research reflexivity as they converge in visual media. Our presentation includes a 5-minute filmlet on loop on a single screen with 1 set of headphones and 1 chair. The filmlet introduces Ambler, the REACH project and some emerging themes.

camra

The Ward: Dubois and Oral Histories

The Ward is a community organization dedicated to promoting W. E. B. DuBois vision for Philadelphia's black community, a vision he developed in the seventh ward when writing The Philadelphia Negro. *The Ward* promotes "public history," by collecting the memories and recollections of the seventh ward's population. They have used this rich archive of personal histories in a variety of ways creating a board game, a school curriculum, a mural, maps and mapping tools, a variety of books and brochures and documentaries, one of which camra helped them to produce.

The installation will provide an interactive space for users to "play" board games as they watch and hear about the life of civil rights activists and religious leaders from the Seventh Ward community. By thinking outside of the book and even outside of the film we seek to think about the many ways that learning (kinesthetic, audiovisual, etc.) can occur and the differential possibilities which tactile interaction might provide for active engagement with "lived" histories, like that of the Seventh Ward community. The Ward's work reminds us that the possibilities for creative generation from archives are not limited to acts of inscription.

camra
Sweet Tea

Sweet Tea, a feature-length experimental/ethnographic documentary, will follow the personal and scholarly trajectory of researcher and activist E. Patrick Johnson. Johnson (the first Black man from his small town of Hickory, North Carolina, to earn a PhD) uses social scientific and humanistic methods to examine questions of identity and community in contemporary society. As someone who has documented his own coming-out story, Johnson also seeks to understand the many different experiences of Black gay men from the South and to share their stories with audiences through both scholarly and artistic means. Most recently, he has transformed his extensive ethnographic life history interviews with gay Black Southerners into a one-man theatrical show, *Sweet Tea*. This ethnographic film (of the same name) will combine footage from the rehearsal and production of that show with documentary moments from the lives of both Johnson and his interview participants, depicting both his research process and the complexities of his relationships with the men in his study. The film, much like Johnson's work itself, attempts to transcend conventional assumptions about what counts as "scholarship"—and to reimagine how such scholarship can/should be shared. How do we represent portions of other people's life stories? How do those stories impact us as researchers and viewers? What does it even mean to blur the boundaries between art and science, scholarship and activism, and what's to be gained from doing so? Sweet Tea, the film, attempts to place these interconnected themes and questions in critical and creative conversation.

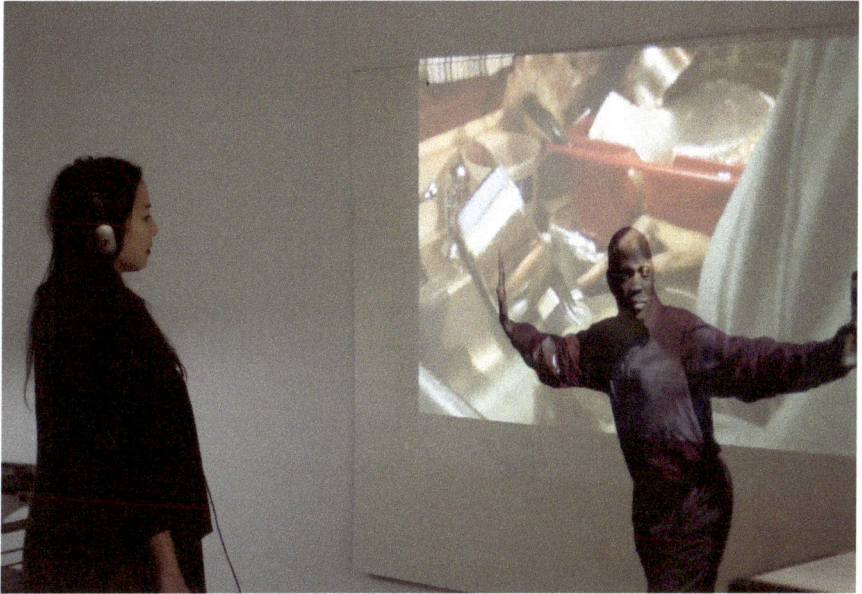

Grayson Cooke
AgX

AgX is an art-science project about material memory and forgetting; it features time-lapse macro-photography of photographic negatives being chemically destroyed.

This project is comprised of two video works. Each work explores the chemical decomposition of photographic negatives via redox reaction, ion exchange and electron transfer. The first work, *HNO3*, presents photographic negatives enveloped in nitric acid, acetic acid, and sulphuric acid. The second work, *H2O2*, uses hydrogen peroxide, copper, silver nitrate and sodium hypochlorite. These processes are digitally photographed over anything from 2 hours to 2 days, and collated into time-lapse video sequences. They have been edited to a soundtrack by sound artist Rafael Anton Irisarri.

The symbol "AgX" is chemical shorthand for the silver halides, the light-sensitive compounds that constitute the celluloid image. The silver halides are the ground of a certain historical regime of the image, its material basis and possibility of signification. But they are also the ground of personal and collective memory – the blood of the modern archive, its pulsing life. As digital imaging comes to play an increasingly large role in personal and collective life, however, the form of the archive, and thus of memory AND forgetting, is changing.

AgX is thus a material enquiry into memory and forgetting, situated at the confluence of analog and digital media. The photographs in this project come from the artist's archive of photographic materials, they record the images of friends, small details, and naïve obsessions of a former time. They are not artistically significant, and are returned to us here as nostalgia, but they are also just things in the world, subject to the same physical and chemical laws as any other body, prone to dissolution and disappearance just as much as to remembrance. *AgX* shows us images transcending their image-ness as they reduce to their material form.

Jean-Robert Dantou and Florence Weber
Objects and constraints

A bent toothbrush, a pipe, a trashbag, an engagement ring, perfume
bottles... A photographer and social scientists sought out objects that
focus on decision-making for people described as suffering from mental
illness.

How can a decision be made when the person in question is described as
being incapable of deciding for themselves ? How can their perspective,
and that of their friends and family, be taken into consideration?
How can it not be taken into consideration? In each case, the dangers
the person faces, as well as the dangers they put others in, have to be
weighed up against jeopardizing their freedom.

The perception of these dangers makes a difference. What are acceptable
risks, unacceptable ones, and for whom ? Each decision brings into
play a combination of experiences, knowledge, perceptions and norms.
These "marker objects" beckon, signal, allow stories to be told that are
intertwined with the lives of those that suffer, those that care for them,
those that love them and live with the uncertainty.

Zohar Kfir
Points of View

Points of View is an ongoing interactive web documentary based on
video footage shot by Palestinians working with B'Tselem's Camera
Distribution Project. It offers an intimate and situated look at life under
the Israeli occupation.

The basis for this documentary project is video footage from B'Tselem,
The Israeli Information Center for Human Rights in the Occupied
Territories. In 2007, B'Tselem began giving Palestinians living in
the West Bank and Gaza video cameras as well as basic training in
shooting and editing. Their hope was that the resulting video would
allow Palestinians themselves to not only document the infringement
of their rights, but also to present their the anger, pain, joy, and hope of
their daily lives to both Israelis and to the international public. Points
of View aims to increase exposure to B'tslem's important and unique
project through the creation of a map based interactive documentary
that both situates the footage in its location of origin and creates new
narrative threads of meaning from the stories that emerge. Viewers can
browse the clips randomly, or follow pre-determined video trails that
are connected via events and tags. The video trails offer viewers a way to
learn more about particular events or areas, but also allow them to make
their own connections, creating non-linear narratives that resist the fixed
conclusions that can be provoked by linear documentary filmmaking.
This user-directed interface empathizes the auto-ethnographic nature
of the video footage, and the lack of a fixed narrative thread allows for
the footage to be seen and understood as a series of insightful yet highly
complex 'snapshots' of a situation that is often stripped of subtlety and
dimension in media accounts.

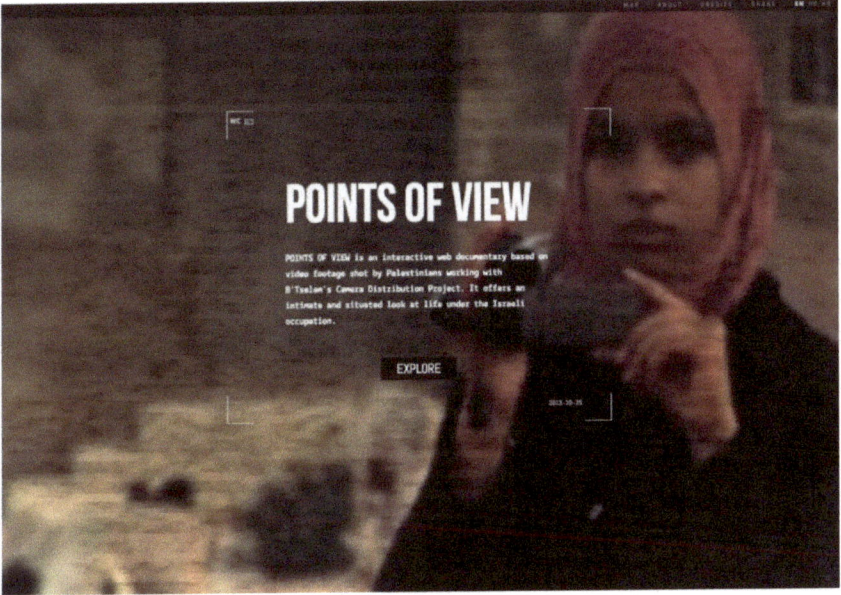

POINTS OF VIEW

POINTS OF VIEW is an interactive web documentary based on video footage shot by Palestinians working with B'Tselem's Camera Distribution Project. It offers an intimate and situated look at life under the Israeli occupation.

EXPLORE

William Odom
Photobox

For over one hundred years, photographs have played a critical role in capturing, representing and provoking discussion on social movements and cultural events. In our world today, the convergence of social, cloud and mobile computing enable people to create archives of digital photographs at larger scales and faster rates than ever before. Facebook now receives 4,000 photo uploads per second, making it the largest photographic archive in human history by orders of magnitude. In an age of high technology, a paradox that philosophers have long debated seems more relevant than ever: if we capture everything, how will we make sense of anything? How will digital photo archives be meaningfully experienced over time, potentially across generations, as they grow to a size and scale never previously encountered? And, what implications might this trend toward rapid digital photo accumulation have for our practices of remembering on personal, social and cultural levels?

Photobox is created to explore and respond to these questions. It is a slow technology intended to be used over many years that occasionally prints a randomly selected photo from its owner's Flickr collection. *Photobox* provokes prolonged periods of reflection on discrete elements in the archive by subverting all control from its owner. Photos are automatically, infrequently and randomly pulled and printed from the archive; they are manifested to explore the casual material durability a photo might offer in contrast to the digital file. In contrast to still accelerating rates of photo accumulation, the Photobox explores opportunities for slowing down consumption of photos, opening a space for pause and reflection, and exploring the dynamics of use and non-use with critical photographic 'display' technologies.

Aga Tamiola
A Story Within and Beyond

In 2013 I collaborated with The Endangered Archives Project at the British Library. EAP rescues collections that may otherwise have been lost. I have looked specifically at a digitalized photographic archive of Siberian indigenous peoples.

I investigated the science of photography at the turn of the 19th and 20th century, as well as the character of ethnographic research of that time. The selection of the glass plate images for the photoetchings was a very difficult one and I wanted through the choices I made to shed some light on how the images were taken in the first place, often in a random way. The prints are an attempt to keep alive the stories of the indigenous peoples of Siberia at the turn of the 20th century.

I worked with the digital archive and I never saw the original glass plate negatives for this particular project. I visited the British Library archive where a lot of glass plate negatives from the time of the British Empire were kept to familiarize myself with the glass plates as objects in their own rights. Making physical prints of the digitalized collection brought new life to a digitalized collection and the glass plate negatives as well.

It would not have been possible to make the prints without the permission of the Krasnoiarsk Regional Museum and the input of anthropologist Craig Campbell.

The project culminated in the prints being shown in the Encounters between Art and Science exhibition at The British Library in London.

Alejandro Luperca Morales
Post Meridiem/ Post Mortem

The disappearance, a dramatic trend that would relate to the poetics of the trace and its gradual fading (Ana Mendieta) or even what Derrida called the ashes, the impossibility to rebuild what is lost, locates the (in) visibility on a strategy to make visible a dehumanized body, due to the aesthetics of the narco-violence where death is no longer the ultimate goal but the breakdown of the body through its postmortem punishment. Here, the relentless visual perception of these falling bodies produces new ways of seeing / escape / interpret reality through media manipulation as a strategy of resistance.

Post meridiem/ Post Mortem, forms a comprehensive visual record of the manual manipulation of the juarense local newspaper PM, where the raw and brutal images of dismembered bodies have been removed with manual processes using rubber erasers directly on the paper substrate. As an uncanny image, the absence of this hyperreal body reveals the journalistic formats that are used in contemporary Mexico.

All of this corpses -invisible others- become visible through its absence. Like the transparency achieved by thinning the paper in these series of newspapers, the artist is alleging a visual alternative that is not governed by the laws of socially instituted vision. To achieve consciousness of what it is photography and what can be photographed and between the discussion of viewers and governments habituated to such horror on a mass scale, we trench on a counter image.

Robert Peterson and Myron Beasley
The Moment of (Ecstatic) Truth in the Translator's Dance

For several years Robert Peterson and Myron Beasley have collaborated on a series of sound projects derived from an archive collected in Port-au-Prince, Haiti, weeks before the earthquake of 2010. At the core of the archive are interviews of five master sculptors that base their operations around Gallerie E Pluribus Unum, a gallery and workshop situated in the center of the bustling city among scrapyards and commercial wood carving operations. Our current fascination is with the gaps that occur in translation during the intercultural interview process. Our proposed project critically interrogates the space between interview narratives and translation. We seek to interrogate the 'lost' in translations as well as what is embellished by the translator. Here the translator is critical as he represents not only someone doing a job, but someone possessed of an idiosyncratic narrative about himself and his culture that he desires to project. The translator lives in the 'significant gaps and blind spots' between cultures which is at the crux of this iteration of the Ethnographic Terminalia project. Recognizing that the area of translation studies is broad and vast in technique and theory speaks to the power given to a translated text. We are interested in the gaps in understanding produced by the performance of the translator as they constitute an 'ecstatic truth' in the interpretation of the narratives. Therefore this project seeks out porous readings of the gaps. The liminal zone that the translator performs in provides a space for play in which the very language being negotiated is called into question on both sides. Through multiple translations layers of truths about what was said and what was meant can come to light and be applied to one another to derive a definition of 'truth' somewhere in the space between the scientist and the poet.

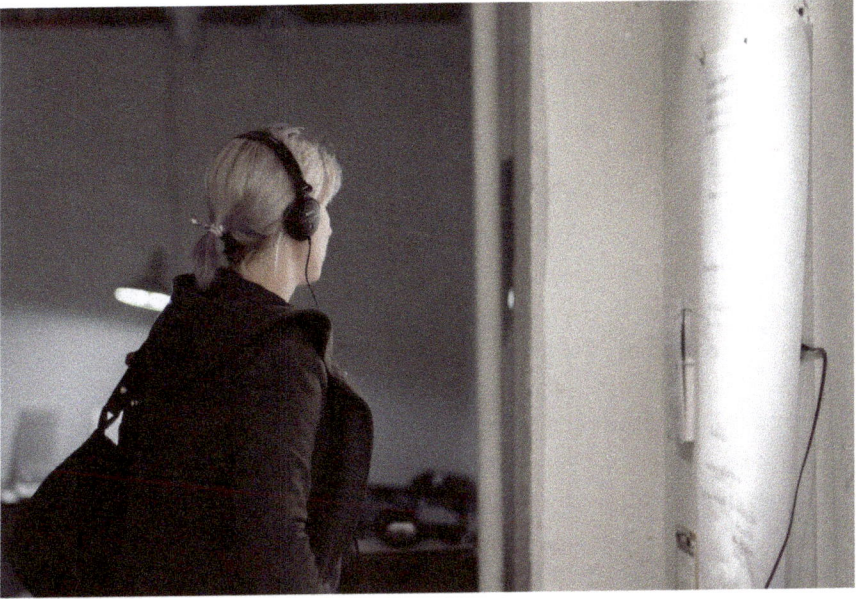

Anna Laine
Making Home: with five artists based in the UK

This video is a collaboration between Anna Laine and the diaspora artists Reginald S. Aloysius, Hari Rajaledchumy, Anushiya Sundaralingam, Sabes Sugunasabesan and Arunthathi Ratnaraj. It conveys how the artists investigate their Tamil Sri Lankan background and current plural belonging through their art practice, how their working processes of dialectic movements between accommodating themselves and creating disruptions take individual as well as shared forms. The complexity of the artists' positions has been explored by means of direct improvisations and constructed settings in London, Belfast and Jaffna, over an eighteen-months' period. They way the artists presently reconnect with fragmented memories, displaced skills, lost objects and confused feelings becomes a means to reimagine both the archive and possible futures.

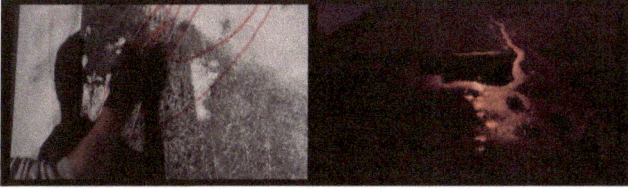

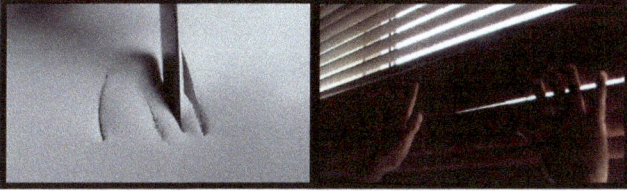

Kwame Phillips and Debra Spitulnik Vidali
Kabusha Radio Remix: Your Questions Answered by Pioneering Zambian Talk Show Host, David Yumba (1923-1990)

This installation repurposes Bemba language analog material from and about one of Zambia's most famous radio personalities. Originally collected in Zambia between 1986 and 1990 by Debra Spitulnik Vidali, it has been digitized for a new initiative entitled the Bemba Online Project (BOP) and for a book project. David Yumba was the creator and producer of the Bemba language radio program Kabusha Takolelwe Bowa, a Bemba proverb meaning "The Person Who Inquires First, Is Not Poisoned by a Mushroom." In the program Yumba answered listeners' letters about politics, society, family, and current events as they were read aloud by co-host Emelda Yumbe. The show ran for more than 25 years on Radio Zambia, up to the time of Yumba's death in 1990, and was one of the most popular radio programs in Zambian radio history. One might think of David Yumba as a Larry King or Michael Moore of the Zambian airwaves, tinged with a bit of Dear Abby or Doctor Ruth in his personal advisory tone, all overlaid by a characteristically Bemba oratorical style of a grandfatherly griot or trickster.

The installation features a remixed and reinvented Kabusha "radio program" produced by Kwame Phillips and Debra Spitulnik Vidali. The remixed version emulates the format of the original 60-minute program. Excerpts of Yumba's answers in past programs are used to answer questions from present-day Bemba archive workers about the politics and technicalities of archives, as well as new questions from "anonymous" letter writers about current Zambian and global politics. As the archived voice of the sage David Yumba is activated to advise a new group of question askers, the installation throws issues of subject agency, immortality, translation, wisdom, and ownership into bold relief.

Christian S. Hammons
In Animate: A Multispecies Ethnography

In Animate: A Multispecies Ethnography, a multimedia (video/film and sculpture) installation, is part of an ongoing project in sensory ethnography at the Carousel of Happiness, a restored carousel in the mountain town of Nederland, Colorado. The project explores the capacity of mimetic machines to animate the inanimate by routinely traversing the human-animal divide. Both the carousel and the cinema are late 19th century technologies with ongoing afterlives in the 21st century. They materialize moments in time. They are both archive and ephemera.

In 1983, still recovering from the trauma of the Vietnam War and plunging into a career handling torture cases for Amnesty International, Scott Harrison began to carve animals. They were larger than life, colorful, and at the time, homeless. Two decades later, more than 30 were scattered throughout the small mountain town of Nederland, Colorado. Then, in 2006, with the support of the community, the animals were brought together under one roof, along with the frame of a 100-year-old Loof carousel and a 1913 Wurlitzer organ. The Carousel of Happiness opened in 2010.

Born from trauma and the creative impulse of a man and a community, the carousel now has a life and a creative impulse of its own. It is a living, breathing organism made of metal and grease, carved wood and paint, people and stories. The installation takes this proposition seriously, using a variety of media, like the carousel, to reverse the polarity of animate and inanimate. At the Carousel of Happiness, the machine – the inanimate – is organic and alive. It animates not only the sculpted animals, but also the humans who ride them, absorbing them and their experience into its frame. It is a collection of human agency, which is itself agent. The carousel is animatic.

Amber Lincoln
History Felt: Alaska Peninsula Reindeer Herding

Over the last two years of research in southwest Alaska, I've developed a feel for the region's history as I've been tracking down the history of reindeer herding on the Alaska Peninsula. At the turn of the 20th century, pastoralism was introduced to northwest Alaska as part of a government program to "improve" the welfare of Alaska natives. This program spread southward to the Alaska Peninsula in 1905. For 45 years, herders ranged as many as 10,000 reindeer throughout the Peninsula, supplying the region with meat and hides. The viability of herding on the Alaska Peninsula, however, was short-lived and ended in 1950. Herders could not afford to miss out on high-paying fishing jobs which took them away from their reindeer, leaving the reindeer to fall prey to wolves or join wild caribou herds.

While this history is not yet easily accessible, some fragments survive: memos, rangeland permits, and maps housed in U.S. National Archives, historical photos and tools in individual collections and museums. Other parts of this history remain protected by their ubiquity among community members, as reindeer stories are told and retold. In this installation I've woven together threads of different media. Specific properties—the design of documents, the texture of objects, the rhythm of voices—animate its underlying data, spanning wide temporal and geographical space to congregate in history making. Feelings of familiarity and estrangement, satisfaction, and disconnection emerge from discovering a single event or person through different modes of awareness: reading, touching, listening. These are the feelings of doing historical ethnography that guide and shape the directions of my research, and provide anchors for analysis.

As a cultural anthropologist, I draw on phenomenology, material culture, and storytelling approaches. I'm fascinated by the things we make, and the processes and narratives involved in making. These interests shape how I explore my current research about the histories and legacies of reindeer herding on the Alaska Peninsula.

Trish Scott
Untitled (Site)

This film examines how the archive, at the intersection of concept and matter, can be understood as a site, and how this can be visualised and given material form. Archives are notoriously tricky to pin down both geographically, temporally and discursively and Untitled (Site) explores the relationship between archival sites(s) and archival experience as mediated via a particular lip synced recording played out in different environments. The work tests whether archives have boundaries, whether it's possible to distinguish archival from non-archival experience, exploring the overlap between discursive and locational sites and the relationship between textual, semantic and sensory experience.

Untitled (Site) grew out of practice based research conducted at the Baring Financial Archive in the City of London. Like all archives, this archive is leaky. It bleeds out of its official storeroom into other spaces within the institution, as well as into digital space, and other conceptual fields. Drawing on Doreen Massey's conception of "spatiotemporal events", in which Massey proposes an event based notion of space that's a product of interrelations, this film moves away from formulating the archive as a site which hosts or stores documents (or a container in which historic material exists and processes happen) to propose a formulation of the archive as an event that's constantly being made and re-made, tracking this via my everyday experience.

Petrina Ng
Heirloom Facsimile

My practice explores the duality of the artefact as simultaneously the archaeological term of a recovered object of cultural significance, as well as the scientific term for an error in perception or representation of information produced by the medium involved.

I am often engaged with the failure and absurdity of attempting to preserve time. I am interested in the creation of legacy and value, and how these things can remain, diminish or be fabricated. The exploration of these ideas hints at a tenuous relationship to our own sense of mortality. My work explores a paradox of memory: by attempting to preserve and monumentalize, we are acknowledging loss.

Objects from my personal or family's archive, such as photographs, texts, videos and other ephemera, are manipulated and re-contextualized to explore broader questions of history and the archive. Material paradoxes are utilized to embody and imitate relationships of unease and familiarity, as well as an unexpected playfulness.

Heirloom Facsimile is a triptych of tapestry panels that re-materialize a three-page public service document issued by a governmental body of Hong Kong. The content of the document recommends approaches of cancer prevention that are largely foreign to western medicine. From a North American perspective, the poorly translated English also reads similarly to a modern chain letter, further alienating a western reading. The original document was faxed and then scanned before it came into my possession and my re-rendering of the original includes the resulting digital noise from these mechanical processes. I have translated each pixel of this digitized document into a single cross stitch, reimagining each page as a 4x-enlarged embroidery panel. The result is a failed attempt to monumentalize an ephemeral document, whilst emphasizing its questionable social, political and cultural utility and authority when viewed by a foreign audience.

Megha Sehdev and Saransh Sugandh
ghar aur kaagaz: Home and Document

Transnational trends in documentary photography have recently taken a "domestic turn", focusing on everyday scenes and objects in home spaces. This newfound attention to domestic objects on the one hand continues an aesthetic preoccupation from the 1990s with commodity culture, shifting critiques of the commodity fetish to an appreciation of the ontological status of everyday objects. Yet, new works also signal that home spaces are no longer hidden from the gaze of surveillance – especially from documentary technologies that reveal our most intimate lives to human voyeurism and digital algorithms. In this photo project, entitled *ghar aur kaagaz* – Hindi for *Home and Document* (or more literally, *Home and Paper*), we mimic documentary photography's use of mundane and everyday "object tableaus". As in the work of Indian documentary photographers Gauri Gill, and Tejal Shah, daily objects come to life as they stand for themselves, affectively charged. However, our images tend to short-circuit this material coherence. Superimposed over the photos is an overpowering discursive form – text from legal domestic violence cases.

The project is a deliberate attempt to combine visualizations of domestic space with meta-level descriptions of domestic space offered by legal writing. It therefore performs the critique of surveillance presumably within current documentary photography – that intimate spaces are open-ended – open to voyeuristic eyes, affects, and sometimes to dangerous interpretations. However, rather than stopping at the "openness" of the image, we show how absurd and melodramatic legal text, in performing a discursive reading – enters back into the frame, creating a moment in which genres, spaces, and objects – become unintelligible and momentarily collapse.

The photos are a series of pictures taken by the artists of domestic spaces in New Delhi. The textual matter has been culled from legal documentation from the anthropologist's (Megha Sehdev's) case studies of domestic violence litigation in the Delhi district courts.

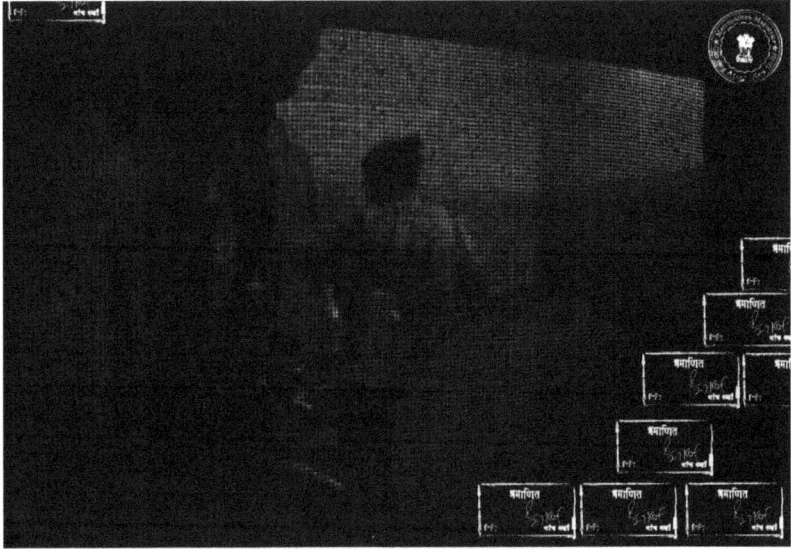

Chitra Venkataramani
Gatekeepers

In 2012, my fieldwork took me to various land record offices and state archives in Mumbai, in order to find information relating to land records and surveys. These documents and maps are notoriously difficult to obtain as most older land records are neither digitized, nor are they catalogued in any explicit order. Instead, they lie in crumbling, forgotten buildings, wrapped up in cloth bundles – both the building and the record slowly disintegrating over time. The impossibility of obtaining specific documents is heightened by the fetishization of the document itself: land and revenue records are deeply tied up with governance and state control.

Throughout my research, I would find myself waiting in these buildings and often simply watching the government workers: Kafkaesque gatekeepers who mediated my access to these records. While I was prepared for the arduous process of waiting to get access, I was not prepared for the proximity with these governmental figures that mediated my relationship to the archive. Every day, this proximity was tinged with uncertainty of different sorts. Not only was I uncertain about whether I would be allowed to access a record on any given day, but also unsure about the form in which my requests would manifest. Many a time, my requests for particular records would yield completely unpredictable results, or manifest as moth eaten documents that would wither upon my touch.

In order to bear this period of proximal, uncertain, and arduous waiting, I began writing and drawing portraits of my gatekeepers and paying attention to the kinds of stamps, signatures, and traces they left upon the documents that passed their desk. My work, which is entitled *Gatekeepers*, works as a "catalogue" of this experience, bringing together a series of portraits, material traces, and government documents, to think about lives of these figures suspended in a diffuse archive. I seek to suggest that these gatekeepers are complex characters whose role extends beyond that of an intermediary.

Alexandrine Boudreault-Fournier and Marie-Josée Proulx
Datatrack

Datatrack is an audio-photo series about the inscriptions and traces, the flows and circulation patterns, the spaces, things and materialities that music and sound files build in the contemporary world. This photo series accompanied by original audio clips explore how three music aficionados from Montreal archive, store, create and keep track of musical data. The photos are visual mise-en-scènes of datatracks. They accentuate the ways in which musical tracks are consumed and archived. Different strategies of conservation are used to archive formatted music (MP3, flac, wav, AAC) in hard drives, on shelves, in folders, and even on walls. Yet, once played, sound and music, are uncontainable and the vibrations are lost in the air like a kite without a chord; they flow and evaporate. The audio clips are sonic mise-en-scènes that interweave music composed by the music aficionados, their voices, ambient sounds and audio effects. The sonic mise-en-scènes amplify the materialities of the data track; intensify the flow and lost of data, and magnify the desire −obsession −to track and keep exaggerated amount of data on a cloud, in one's pocket, or on an external hard drive. *Datatrack* refers to how people actively keep track of their data even if in a context of digital superabundance users often lose track of where is the data, of what it contains, and to whom it belongs. *Datatrack* is a wink to the unique strategies we invent to stop the leaking of containment and conservation of data.

The photos and the sound clips were collected in the context of the ethnographic MusDig research project based at the University of Oxford and funded by the European Research Council.

Tim Schwartz
Botanical Loss

These prints represent what was lost as a series of early botanical prints
was converted into a contemporary "lossless" image format and archived
online. In 1799, Robert John Thornton released the first installment
of the book The Temple of Flora, the first large color floral volume
ever published. Inspired by Linnaeus, the founder of modern botany,
Thornton set out to represent the newly discovered sexual systems of
plants through commissioned paintings. Only a few of these original
copies still exist including a copy that resides at the Missouri Botanical
Garden Research Library, one of the largest botanical libraries in the
country. A number of years ago Taschen approached the library to
make a new edition. After making very high quality scans for Taschen,
the library converted the files to JPEG2000 (a lossless JPEG format)
and uploaded them as archival web quality images to the Biodiversity
Heritage Library online.

A piece of software has been written to compare the high quality scan
of the book and the digital online surrogates pixel by pixel. If the color
values of the same pixel from the two files are the same, the produced
pixel is black. If the pixels are different, the color difference is produced.
These images, the result of doing this for all pixels, represent the color
shift or loss in quality between the two files.

Xinyuan Wang
Bottled Factory Workers

How to archive 'sound' in a more engaging and contextual way? This work employs the factory sounds which the ethnographer Xinyuan Wang recorded in the factory where her informants worked and she lived for 15 months. It is a combination of the real-life sounds with images of the factory workers. Just like the factory where those rural migrants work and the place where they live, the small space of the glass bottle is stuffed with people and filled with noise. Factories not only produce goods but also 'factory workers'. No matter who you are, where you come from, and why you are happy or upset, one's personal stories and emotions are overwhelmed and flooded by the roar of machines on the assembly line and the scale of the factory itself. So in this exhibit we find them crammed into a mass of other people and deafening sounds.

Raul Ortega Ayala
18 and a half minutes

18 and half minutes is part of a group of works that explore the concept
of Social Amnesia and the politics behind memory through research and
visual representation. During the research I came across the infamous
case of the tape where a conversation between Nixon and his chief
of staff, Bob Haldeman, was abruptly erased for 18 and half minutes.
This removal of information caught my attention because it illustrated
an explicit intervention in collective memory. In the transcripts of the
Watergate trial found in the Nixon Presidential Library Archives the
explanations as to why this gap occurred, differ greatly. Nixon told the
grand jury that his secretary, Rose Woods, had told him that she had
damaged the recording but only briefly. Then the former president said
that General Alexander Haig, his security adviser, informed him that
18 and half minutes of conversation had been erased from the tape.
Further in the transcripts he suggests that the taping machine had
malfunctioned. In another version Woods says that the president came
into the room and began "pushing the buttons back and forth" and in a
testimony in November 1973, she denied responsibility: "The buttons
said on and off, forward and backward. I caught on to that fairly fast. I
don't think I'm so stupid as to erase what's on a tape".

Although we will never know what was said in that room, nor the true
circumstances of the tape's erasure, the 18 and half minutes of white
noise nevertheless say a lot. They reflect a deliberate attempt to modify
the record of events and symbolize the significance of erasure and gaps
in the construction of History.

With this research in mind and with the actual static on the tape I
made a prototype for a public sculpture to remember this event and to
symbolize the many things that go unsaid in history.

The Schizophonic Archive

The Schizophonic Archive is comprised of three interrelated projects exploring recorded sound, residual media, and archives.
Stairwell: Lina Dib with Navid Navab
Schizo-Phone: Craig Campbell with Katie Van Winkle, Julián Etienne, Juan Pablo González, Vasilina Orlova, Nora Tyeklar, Tamara Becerra Valdez and Hallie Boas
Radio Sets: Tom Miller with David Goren

"Modern memory is, above all, archival. It relies entirely on the materiality of the trace…" - Pierre Nora
Schizophonia, def. The separation of sounds from their sources

The Schizophonic Archives highlight the roles machines play in making the ephemeral tangible and repeatable. Within the Bureau of Memories were stations where visitors listened through radios, telephones, and sensors to transient fragments culled from a vast ocean of ethnographic and other sound archives.

There are three components to *The Schizophonic Archive*:

• Machines for Transforming Time into Matter: As visitors entered and exited the gallery space via the main stairwell, their movements triggered familiar sounds of recently obsolete inscription devices. Each passage up or down the staircase produced a different combination of sounds.
• The Schizo-Phone, a specially reinvented telephone receiver, allows listeners to call up archival sound fragments from deep ethnographic archives by dialling the appropriate number to listen in on the past. Antique radio sets placed at intervals throughout the gallery continually broadcast fragments and remixes of field recordings, decaying wax cylinders, and short-wave propaganda broadcasts.
The accompanying guidebooks included information, images, and enigmas related to the polyphonic traces of voices, machines, and static flickering across the soundscape of the Bureau of Memories.

We would like to recognize Conaculta's Fonoteca Nacional for permission to use materials from their archive.

A junior member of the Ethnographic Terminalia
curatorial collective considers her research materials

www.ingramcontent.com/pod-product-compliance
Lightning Source LLC
Chambersburg PA
CBHW040138270326
41927CB00020B/3438